BRING ME THE HEAD OF THE TASKMASTER

BRING ME THE HEAD OF THE TASKMASTER

101 Next Level Tasks (And Clues)
To Lead You To Victory

Fastest wins.
Your time starts now.

'I believe in second chances, but I don't believe in third or fourth chances'

S. Gomez

3 5 7 9 10 8 6 4 2

Ebury Spotlight, an imprint of Ebury Publishing
20 Vauxhall Bridge Road,
London SW1V 2SA

Ebury Spotlight is part of the Penguin Random House group of companies whose addresses can be found at global.penguinrandomhouse.com

This book is published to accompany the television series entitled *Taskmaster* first broadcast on Dave in 2015, subsequently broadcast on Channel 4 in 2020. *Taskmaster* is an Avalon production.

First published by Ebury Spotlight in 2021
Paperback edition first published by Ebury Sportlight in 2022

www.penguin.co.uk

A CIP catalogue record for this book is available from the British Library

ISBN 978 1 529 14844 2

Commissioning editor: Yvonne Jacob
Project editor: Daniel Sorensen
Design: Clarkevanmeurs Design Ltd
Illustrations: Richard Palmer
Production: Catherine Ngwong

Printed and bound in Great Britain by Clays Ltd, Elcograf S.p.A.

The authorised representative in the EEA is Penguin Random House Ireland, Morrison Chambers, 32 Nassau Street, Dublin DO2 YH68

Penguin Random House is committed to a sustainable future for our business, our readers and our planet. This book is made from Forest Stewardship Council® certified paper.

CONTENTS

FOREWORD
BY GREG DAVIES

When Alex told me he wanted to write a second *Taskmaster* book my initial response was a firm 'no'. It's not that I was against the idea in principle, I just find that Alex is a man who thrives on firmly maintained boundaries.

If I were to say yes to every flight of fancy he conjures up in his awful little shed then he might become the preening show pony that rears its ugly nose from time to time on the show. Please don't think that the fact you have the book in your hand means there has been any softening on my part.

In order to get the go-ahead Alex had to complete several of his own little 'tasks'. Thus what you are about read was written in complete isolation within the confines of a building in my garden. Alex was allowed only candle-light, and lived on supermarket vitamins and white bread for the duration of his writing period.

I allowed a local farmer to enter the (for the sake of succinctly putting it) compound after eight weeks. Alex was waxed/sheared from head to foot and dusted with mite formula. On week 13 I was presented with the first draft. I immediately destroyed it in a garden incinerator whilst he watched on. I made it clear to him that I hadn't read so much as a word and was doing this for his own good.

That he had to go through this process six further times before I accepted draft one of what you are about to read is a lesson for him and each and everyone of you.

Tasks are serious and should be taken seriously. Approach each of the ones contained in this book as if it is the last thing you will ever do. If you are tackling the infuriatingly fiddly treasure hunt, be aware that it will take over your life. It's far too hard. Even when you've solved all the clues – which, he assures me, you will eventually – you'll then have to work out how they relate to a grid at the back of the book. It's a nightmare. He's a nightmare. But he's my nightmare.

And so, as I type the next sentence I am howling the words aloud; the haunting screech of a mighty bird of prey: over to little Alex Horne ...

WELCOME TO THE PAPERBACK READERS

This is an important message for readers of the paperback version of this book (if you can see this sentence, that means you are a reader of the paperback version, so do read on). This message does not appear in the hardback version of this book for the very good reason that this message was not written for the hardback (nor could it have been), but for the paperback only. It is a message exclusive to this version and cannot be found anywhere else, which makes it a tiny bit special.

Firstly, welcome. Secondly, there is some news. Not bad news exactly, but news nonetheless. The fact is, by the time paperback readers read this book, the search for the coveted Silver Head will be over. That priceless artefact will by now be proudly displayed in the home of the successful Hunter, or perhaps secured in a high security safe, or, if it was unexpectedly found by Kerry Godliman, it will likely be lying face down somewhere in her garage.

Regardless, that Hunt is over. But here is some more news: while it was really lovely that someone did manage to locate Greg's magnificent head, many, many people had a fantastic time participating in the Hunt, even if they were not the ultimate victor.

It's important to remember that the Hunt itself is more important than the Head itself. And that is where this book comes in: it gives you, the new Hunter, or a veteran Hunter who fancies another go with added help, the chance to experience the Hunt without having the constant stress of whether or not you'll find the Head. Because you won't. As I said, it's already been found. But you can still complete the Hunt, which in itself is something wonderful, and your journey to the wonderfulness of a solid completion of a giant, multi-faceted task will be just as wonderful. And probably a little infuriating. But that's why this paperback comes equipped with things the hardback did not come equipped with: clues. More on that in a moment.

For now, let's focus on the joys of the Hunt. For many months many committed Hunters spent many hours attempting to solve the many riddles and puzzles set for them by my Lord and Daddy, the Taskmaster. A lot of the time they came up with the right answers. Eventually. Before that, they discovered the pure delight of rabbit holes. As you embark on your Hunt, you should be very careful of rabbit holes, although you will almost definitely fall into some, so don't worry too much. When you do discover one, just enjoy the ride.

Some of the rabbit holes Hunters fell into during their Hunt were hugely impressive in their magnificent scope. Even Greg himself can't have foreseen just how deep he could drag people below the surface, but he took great satisfaction in the webs they weaved for themselves and then got stuck in, making such Hunters both spiders *and* prey simultaneously. He loves that sort of stuff.

One particularly thorny stage of the Hunt seemed to send people swirling into all manner of abysses, some of which certain Hunters have kindly allowed me to detail here:

- Paul Green developed an elaborate theory based on time and numbers that involved space missions to the moon and the astronauts involved, minus one who didn't walk on the moon. It was very wrong, but it must've been fun to get there.
- Paul also joined forces with fellow Hunter Kristen McAllister to impressively link elements of the puzzle to Mel Giedroyc's Exotic Sandwich from Series 4 (you may remember it: Mel managed to get an M&M lodged in her nose during one ill-fated bite). Not content with the depth of that hole, Kristen disappeared down another, even deeper hole that eventually led

her to a single crossword which happened to feature 'Taskmaster' as an answer. From here she developed a theory based on stars that was not even close to the solution. 'If this is wrong,' she wrote plaintively, 'I'm actually going to cry myself to sleep tonight.' So that wasn't a pleasant email to respond to. But, unfortunately, that is my job, so reply to it I did.

- Darren Hodson emailed to suggest that the Silver Head might be buried in Jupiter's red eye. Sadly, it wasn't. The closest any of Greg's valuable heads have been to Jupiter is of course the time Ed Gamble sent his trophy into space in search of five precious Champion of Champions points.
- Sisters Sherilyn and Stephanie Yao went very technical on a theory that involved the 'unicode for the geographical concept of spherical angle.' The answer was not to be found there.
- And Karen Hird's thoughts took her on a wild ride from painter Piet Mondrian to George Orwell's 1984, but her voyage to find a shortcut to the Silver Head was even stranger: a German word buried in this book caused her to leap into a German Taskmaster-related rabbit hole, where she made all kinds of inferences inspired by the excellent German comedian, journalist and broadcaster, Carsten van Ryssen and his Wikipedia page. This did not help in the location of the Silver Head, but it did enlarge Karen's knowledge of German entertainment, and, as she asked me to include the details of that rabbit hole in the next Taskmaster book (which is this one), the entire pointless exercise could certainly be said to have had a point in the end.

If all that sounds daunting, do not be daunted. There was no intention to daunt, only an intention to show the hours of fun people have had in trying to solve this conundrum wrapped in many riddles. Also, as mentioned, this paperback comes with clues, which should help to lessen any daunt and also limit the depths of the rabbit holes you find yourselves scrabbling about in like discombobulated bunnies.

You can find those clues at the back of this book and you are free to consult them whenever you like. No one will think anything less of you for doing so. It's not even their business. And there's no need for anyone to know, anyway. It can be your secret. Not a guilty secret, a nice secret. Because clues are nice, everyone likes clues. The clues cover both the many questions and riddles and enigmas within this book, but also the parts of the Hunt that will take you outside this book on a magical trail towards your ultimate goal of being one of the people to reach the end, which will give you a sense of accomplishment not far off that felt by the likes of Widdicombe, Tarbuck, Gamble and Duker as they each reached the pinnacle of their lives when they became Taskmaster champions.

The clues section will also make it clear that the whole Hunt has now been fully automated, meaning you can complete the Hunt as fast as you like. That's another perk of being a paperback Hunter. The hardback Hunters were often left on tenterhooks as they waited for clues to drop, but you have been spared those hooks. Each clue will lead seamlessly to the next with the only thing holding you back being your own detective skills and, perhaps more acutely, the time you have to spare away from your everyday life.

Once the Hunt for The Silver Head begins, be prepared for where it might take you. For Matt Hoskin, the intoxication of trying to solve the hunt with his girlfriend Eleanor led them to decide to get married. Cody and Kara found themselves producing an astounding piece of edible art that featured the face of my beloved Taskmaster. Derek Gould, to help calm himself during the toughest times of the Hunt, set up a Twitter account, @GregsShinyHead, that imagined where the Silver Head might be buried. Here are some examples, but follow him for more wrong answers:

- The Taskmaster's Head might be, but probably isn't, in another castle. Sorry. But like it's always gonna be that way. A bigger castle with tougher turtles protecting it. Good luck!
- The Taskmaster's Head might be, but probably isn't, in the furthest chamber of a dark cave a few leagues north of Phandalin. The door seals behind you as you enter and your passive perception lets you know the floor is uneven. You hear a ticking sound.
- The Taskmaster's Head might be, but probably isn't, drifting down the Nile on a lovely steam-powered river boat. What a beautiful tragedy-free vacation!

Meanwhile, Rachel Baverstock found a release valve in the form of poetry and sent me one correct answer (redacted here, of course) in beautiful verse:

Breakfast time for calves today was running rather late
Because last night my mind ran wild, it was in quite a state
Twas half one before I finally went to bed
But now the chores are done and the calves are fed.

Whilst mucking out and scraping up the poo
I had another thought about what we must do
My head was full of camels, Bedouin tents and sand
But if it's not the desert, the mountains or the land

Maybe it is water, the special place we seek
Perhaps a river, a brook, a stream or maybe a creek
But [redacted] is the spot we sought
Not the sandy deserts which is what I first thought.

Now looking forward to the next clue
With cryptic instructions to tell us what to do.

The Hunt even helped change my own life as one puzzle saw some Hunters utilise their impressive detective skills to put me in touch with some kind people I had been searching for for many years. The first time I found them felt lucky, this time also felt lucky, but in a different way.

The important thing is: have fun. If it does all get too much, or too time-consuming, and you find yourself puzzle-solving when you should be doing something arguably more important, like washing, I suggest following in the sensible footsteps of Zoe and Mya Kempf-Harris's mum. Harbouring concerns treasure hunting might take up more time than their important studies at university, Mum Kempf-Harris took control of the book herself and rationed the clues, drip-feeding them three at a time, like a mummy bird regurgitating semi-digested insects into the mouths of her hungry chicks. I chose that image because that is how Greg feeds me at Saturday tea time before he locks me in my Sunday Room.

Finally, don't forget the Tasks. Because there are Tasks in this book too, and Tasks are what brought us here. Read them, attempt them, enjoy them.

Make good choices.

THE ENDGAME

This is a race.

It is not a race against the clock, because that would be a far easier race. Clocks can be fast, but clocks never win races. It's nearly always humans, sometimes horses and occasionally dogs.

This is a race against your fellow Taskmaster players.

You are competing against everyone else who is reading this book. Some of them are reading this sentence at the exact same time as you. Some of them read it weeks ago. Others haven't even learnt to read yet. You should beat those guys.

All you've got to do is find The Taskmaster's Head first.

You may well be tempted to skip through this bit and start searching for The Taskmaster's Head right away but be warned: you need to read every page of this book; every page might be crucial to finding the prize. This is no straightforward race. This is not 100 metres in a straight line. It's not even a marathon.

This is a race with many twists and turns, that requires very little running, much sideways thinking and quite a lot of patience.

Thankfully, there will be a shedload of tasks along the way to distract you. These tasks will not help you find His Head. They do not contain clues. Like *Taskmaster* itself, they are just for fun. Each one is a distraction that may slow you down, and that is seldom a bad thing. As always, enjoy them, do your best, make good choices.

So what is The Taskmaster's Head?

It's a great question and one that I need to answer immediately before someone attempts to lop off the actual head from The Actual Taskmaster's Body and I regret some of the decisions I've made over the past few months.

The Taskmaster's Head is a white gold replica of His Actual Head. It is actual size. It is beautiful. And it is made of fibreglass and painted silver.

There is only one such Taskmaster's Head in existence. It has been secreted in a location only I am aware of. And it's now up to you to find it.

The first to find it will, of course, keep it, because of the first commandment: Finders Keepers.

But even after the first finder has taken it home, placed it on display, beside their bed, atop their Christmas tree or in their garage, like Kerry Godliman, the game remains afoot. The next hundred to track down The Head's location will also receive something to mark their efforts. And even after that, I will make sure that anyone who successfully uses this map to get to the correct destination is duly rewarded in some way or another.

So get going. Take on the tasks. There are twenty to get you started by yourself right away. But whenever you have a spare second, look at the clues, work out the answers then seek The Taskmaster's Head. Anyone can do it. You can do it. As always with *Taskmaster*, you just have to do the task with *the leitmotiv to remember being crucial: All the information is in the book*.

'The Taskmaster Head shall see you look in every nook'

Walt Milikis

Tasks to do
by yourself

TASK #1

Design your own logo.

Your logo must represent the you that only you know.

Your time starts now.

Clue #1

Dennis, ?, Adefope, Giedroyc, Fielding.

Answer ....

TASK #2

Go for a walk.

Your walk must be exactly 1,000, 2,000, 5,000 or 10,000 steps.

You must then walk exactly the same number of steps back and return to your starting point.

But you must not step anywhere that you stepped before.

You have unlimited attempts.

Your time starts now.

Clue #2

I was borrrn in 1952, I wearrr a neckerrrchief and I'm a big cat.

Answer ....

TASK #3

Write a full length song.

Your time starts now.

They say everyone has a book in them. I think that's quite a reach. But I do think everyone has a song in them. I've made half a living being the singer in a band and I don't have a musical bone in my body. Sit at a piano and press the keys with one finger till you hear something you like. Play a rhythm on your thighs. Write down the words you want to sing. You might surprise yourself.

Clue #3

Something comes first. What comes first?

Answer ....

TASK #4

Close one eye, tilt the book so that it is horizontal and perpendicular to your nose, and look at it from the page number upwards.

Clue #4

What is on my socks? (I do now have muddled up giant arms, so have a look there.)

Answer ....

TASK #5

Write to ten friends that you've not written to before.

See how many letters you get back.

Your time starts now.

Clue #5

This clown belongs to the person who has been on TV more than anyone else (70,000 hours!)

Answer ....

TASK #6

Write ten postcards and leave them in books in your local library.

Leave gaps for other people to write a reply to your message on the postcard.

Check the cards after a year to see how many replies you get back.

Your time starts now.

Clue #6

Little Jack Horner couldn't sit in this cold house.

Answer ....

TASK #7

Paint the following message on a pebble, insert a location of your choice and leave the pebble on your favourite bench:

"I am a pebble and I want to see the world.

Please take me to the bench ____________"

Check the new location whenever possible.

See how many goes it takes for a pebble to hitch a lift and see how far you can make a pebble travel.

Your time starts now.

Clue #7

TV'S TV'S TVTV: Tim masters hula hooping. But what's wearing a white hat?

Answer ....

TASK #8

Be proud of the logo you created for Task #1.

Make your logo visible to as many people as possible.

Have fun with your logo.

Your time starts now.

Clue #8

?, Easte, Futur, Indus, Medie, Ocean.

Answer ....

TASK #9

Make a two minute video for aliens.

Upload your video to YouTube.

Your video should explain what's going on here on Earth in case any aliens are trying to find out.

Best video and first response from an actual alien wins.

Your time starts now.

Clue #9

According to Twitter, where *exactly* is our thwarted potato thrower from?

Answer ....

TASK #10

Design, construct and demonstrate as many of the following as you are able:

1. Windscreen wipers for a pair of glasses.*

2. A machine to put suncream on your own back.

3. A ten minute guide to whistling loudly with your fingers.

4. Food gloves: gloves that have all the functions of knives, forks and spoons that you can wear and then put in the dishwasher.

5. A pocket picnic chair.

6. A fully working velcro business suit.

7. A good beard wig.

8. The kitchen Olympics.

9. Waterproof food that you can eat in the bath.

10. X-ray glasses that actually work, with wind-screen wipers on.

Your time starts now.

*I know they exist. I always wanted a pair when I was a child but they always seemed to be out of stock. So now I want you to make me some.

Clue #10

7 = Snow (71), 25 = ? (76), 39 = Slow (78)

Answer ....

TASK #11

Make a tree, in all its splendour.

Take your time.

Enjoy your splendid tree.

Your time starts now.

Clue #11

Answer ....

TASK #12

Work out how to do at least one of these things to a basic level, one to a good level and one to a genuinely impressive level:

1. **Origami**
2. **Juggling**
3. **Massage**
4. **Astrology**
5. **Darts**
6. **Mind-reading**
7. **Caricatures**
8. **Baking**
9. **Birdwatching**
10. **Magic**

Your time starts now.

Clue #12

A version of my name that people ask a lot of.

Answer ....

TASK #13

Choose an animal. It could be your pet. If you don't have a pet it might have to be an insect that you find or a bird that you see.

Do exactly what your animal does for as long as possible.

Choose another animal and see if you can beat your score.

Your time starts now.

Clue #13

My latest neologism for money.

Answer ....

TASK #14

Do some of these science experiments.

Try, fail, try again, don't worry if it doesn't work, have another go, sit back, be proud of yourself.

Make a windsock so you can see how strong the wind is and where it's coming from.

Try to remember what chromatography is and how to demonstrate it.

Invent a solar powered something.

Do something with a dynamo.

Make a rocket.

Clue #14

(180 x ∃) + (270 x <) + (90 x ɯ) – Who am I?

Answer ....

TASK #15

Choose a wall that you are allowed to mark (chalk and an outside wall might be best).

For an entire year, every time you do the following things, make a Tally mark on your wall.*

1. Sneeze

2. See a squirrel

3. See a rainbow

4. See a hot air balloon

5. Sleep for more than nine hours in one go

6. Fall over

7. Eat more than one bag of crisps in one day

8. Get far too hot

9. Get far too cold

10. Do a really nice thing

Your time starts now.

It'll be interesting, at the very least, to see if you see more rainbows than you fall over.

Next year, see if you can beat your scores.

*A Tally mark is the sort of counting people in prison do in cartoons. It involves making a short vertical line every time something happens. Then when you get to four, your fifth line is a diagonal line across them to make a sort of gate. That gate represents five things and you can start on your next gate.

Clue #15

(A small word in these on page 56 that is sometimes big)

Answer ....

TASK #16

Make some modern art on a proper canvas.

Paint your children, partner or parents.

Go to the top of a hill and paint the view.

Hang your works of art where everyone can see them.

Your time starts now.

Clue #16

Answer ....

TASK #17

Learn to play one piece of music well on one musical instrument.

If you've learnt an instrument in the past, pick it up again and master that song.

For example:

Guitar: 'Back in Black'

Piano: 'Hallelujah'

Recorder: 'Baby Shark'

Harmonica: 'Ain't No Sunshine'

Violin: 'Eye of the Tiger'

Your time starts now.

Clue #17

This Ed joined the Horne Section on July 2nd, 2021.

Answer ....

TASK #18

Grow your hair long if your hair is short.

Dye your hair pink if your hair isn't pink.

Do both of those things to your fingernails if you don't have any hair.

Try it once.

You might like it.

And if you don't, it doesn't matter.

Your time starts now.

Clue #18

The first word of Charlotte and Joe's blurry song.

Answer ....

TASK #19

Without looking at a map, draw the country you are currently in.

Your country should be no more than 1cm long.

Now add an X on the country to show where you are.

Now draw a circle with a diameter of 10cm around your country.

Now add the other countries that surround your country.

Now add the planets that surround your country.

Label everything, including yourself.

Your time starts now.

Clue #19

Answer ....

TASK #20

Record an audiobook for a friend.

Pick your favourite book and read it outloud into some sort of recording device.

Imagine having your friend read you out a whole book: that's what you're doing for them.

Your time starts now.

Clue #20

A boy plays a harmonica, a girl smokes and a couple kiss. There's a fire and a guitar. Another boy is smoking AND drinking and smiling at another girl who is smiling back at him. But when he goes to talk to her she runs away. He asks her her name. She says it's Chrissie.

Answer ....

THE MEAT

There are 101 tasks in this book. It's a good number, 101, for many reasons. It's fun to say. Of course it is. It's palindromic, which is always a laugh.

101 is the first of the numbers to include the letter A, which is both creditable and exactly the sort of fact I always seem to have in my head: There are no 'a's in the first 100 numbers. Brilliant and useless. *And if those numbers were alphabetical they'd start with eight and eighty and end, more importantly, with twenty-two and two.* So now you know too.

Thanks to Orwell's *Nineteen Eighty-Four* 101 is also a famous room – well, torture chamber, if we're being picky. It's the number for the police (if you're in Belgium). It's a whole load of spotty dogs, an album by Depeche Mode and lucky in Hinduism.

But for me it represents the sort of book I want this to be.

101 Jokes For Kids, *101 So Bad, They're Good Dad Jokes*, *101 Fishing Jokes*, those were the books that kept me happy growing up. On every page there was something. They lodged in my head with my facts, I passed them on to my friends and family, and I kept going back for more. My *101 Joke Books* were the most thumbed of all the books of my childhood. And no small part of that was, I'm sure, down to the number itself. There weren't 99 jokes. This wasn't a 99p rip off. There were triple figure jokes in these books. Hang on, no, we're hearing there were even more than that. One hundred and one. And that one was crucial.

So here, for you, are 101 tasks. Share them with the people you know, revisit them, read them over again. Don't count them though. Just in case.

Tasks
for friends
and family

TASK #21

PART ONE

Agree amongst yourselves which is the least loved room in your house.

You have three minutes.

Your time starts now.

PART TWO

Turn the least loved room in your house into the most loved room in the house.

You have one month.

Your time starts now.

Clue #21

I saw this bird on May 7, 2006, in Elmley. Duncton saw one in Dunkeld that year. Their eggs are cream-coloured with brown and reddish spotting and their cry is a shrill "yewk yewk".

Answer ....

TASK #22

Your Taskmaster must choose a book at random for each contestant, and then open those books at random pages.

Write and perform a brand new Christmas Carol using a traditional tune but only words from the page chosen by your Taskmaster.

When you perform your brand new Christmas Carol you must smile manically throughout.

You have ten minutes.

Best Christmas Carol wins.

Clue #22

This guy would have been the 18th storm in 2016 but never made it.

Answer ....

TASK #23

Get the phrase "Handsome Herbert" into circulation.

Start with your family and friends then get more ambitious.

At the time of writing "Handsome Herbert" yields just 1,260 results on Google. We can double that at least, I'm sure.

Your time starts now.

Clue #23

This Gordon got a buzz playing R with Orville and C with Garry.

Answer ....

TASK #24

Everyone should make three paper aeroplanes.

Everyone should go to the top of a hill.

Everyone should throw their paper aeroplanes at least ten times each.

Longest distance by a paper aeroplane wins.

Clue #24

What do these go in?

Answer ....

TASK #25

Build a proper go-kart.

Test your go-kart.

Make your go-kart better.

Test your go-kart again.

Have fun with your go-kart.

Your time starts now.

Clue #25

The sixth champion wrote a book the year before she won. On page 150 she inadvertently wrote the first name of one of the contestants in the next series. It'll give you a real boost.

Answer ....

TASK #26

Make a line of 101 stones, each one larger than the last.

Fastest wins.

Your time starts now.

Clue #26

Feather Pot Feathers Stool Loaf.

Answer ....

TASK #27

Make your signature family fun cocktail.

Your signature family fun cocktail must be so fun.

It must also contain no fewer than ten different ingredients.

You have plenty of time.

Most delicious family fun cocktail wins.

Your time starts now.

Clue #27

Jake Snake had the third best English one in 2011. The Task Consultant and I discovered him at the Windsor Castle but you'd now have to go to The Heron in Paddington.

Answer ....

TASK #28

Communicate in languages other than English for an entire meal.

Last to speak English wins.

Clue #28

The Horne Section's Grandaddy would never do this down to Grade D peas.

Answer ....

TASK #29

Build a communication device between two rooms.

The further apart the rooms and the more ambitious the device the better.

Your communication device must not rely on mobile phones.

If you complete this task you should probably try to build a communication device between two houses.

Your time starts now.

Clue #29

Answer ....

TASK #30

Build the largest reconstruction of a famous landmark.

You have two weeks (or whatever feels right).

Your time starts now.

Clue #30

Vegas' team's German sister.

Answer ....

TASK #31

Record a story on the voicenotes of your phone.

Your story must be no more than three minutes long.

You have ten minutes in total.

When you've all finished, sit quietly and listen to your stories.

Your time starts now.

Clue #31

Our very clever boy had his own Netflix Special. At one point he pretends to be positively what about the drumming on a Coldplay album?

Answer ....

TASK #32

Gather the ingredients you need to make a Christmas cracker:

Toilet roll tubes • A4 Paper

Sticky Tape • Scissors • Ribbon

Ideally something that goes bang

Make a Christmas cracker and put the most surprising thing inside it.

You have one hour.

The thing that surprises your Taskmaster most wins.

Your time starts now.

Clue #32

What font is this?

Answer ....

TASK #33

Pull off the most ambitious dance routine to the most unlikely music.

You have twenty minutes.

Your time starts now.

Clue #33

The last killer in the Belgian books.

Answer ....

TASK #34

Make the best short story out of book titles in your house.

You have ten minutes.

Your time starts now.

Clue #34

What they call you in Nato.

Answer ....

TASK #35

Everyone must tightly tie a towel around their waist before the Taskmaster reads the next instruction.

Without touching your towel with your hands, fold your towel as neatly as possible in one minute.

Most neatly folded towel wins.

Your time starts now.

Clue #35

This fish is not a fish but it is related to a tiger and it walks under water and it used to have the head of a dog and it's Mexican.

Answer ....

TASK #36

Each person should have a sheet of A4 paper.

Make a hole in your paper and get your whole body through the hole.

Fastest wins.

Your time starts now.

Clue #36

Met a met a met a met a.

Answer ....

TASK #37

Successfully hide the biggest thing on your person.

You have four minutes then the Taskmaster will inspect each of you for thirty seconds.

Biggest unfound thing wins.

Your time starts now.

Clue #37

??K596

Answer ....

TASK #38

Pin the moustache on the Taskmaster.

Everyone should have a roll of some sort of tape and a blindfold.

Your Taskmaster must lie on the floor.

Everyone has three minutes to make their Tape Moustache.

Each person, one by one and blindfolded, then has 30 seconds to pin their Tape Moustache on your Taskmaster.

Best moustache and positioning wins.

Your time starts when you're all ready.

Clue #38

You should probably listen to the episode of the Official Taskmaster Podcast in which the ninth champion is joined by someone from *Bridgerton*.

Answer ....

TASK #39

Sit in silence for four hours.

The person who makes their first noise closest to the four hour mark wins.

OR

Don't look at a phone, iPad or laptop.

Last person to look at a phone, iPad or laptop wins.

(ideally both)

Your time starts now.

Clue #39

Where #100 was found.

Answer ....

TASK #40

Everyone must get a cushion, then:

Throw your cushion the furthest.

Starting with the person in the lead, each person in turn must throw their cushion from wherever they like.

The first person must throw their cushion in one minute from now and the next person must throw a minute after them.

Furthest throw wins.

Your time starts now.

Clue #40

Answer ....

THE APPLE

If I am to become The Taskmaster myself one day, to sit on that slightly larger throne next to a golden semi-likeness of my own head, I know I must improve. I would like nothing more than to become the second Taskmaster but there is so much work to be done.

My hero growing up was the singular Dutchman, Pieter Mondriaan. The second of his parents' children, he started slowly but worked hard and eventually bloomed. It can be done.

When he was about my age he moved to Paris and dropped three letters from his name so that he could become an anagram: I paint modern: Piet Mondrian (he also did a sort of 'map rendition'). He had the Spanish Flu and survived. He liked to dance and his home was full of his own works of art. He was my kind of guy.

He was cool, Piet. He may have specialised in straight lines, but he never used a ruler. I want to be like Mondrian. I can do it. I want to do it. See below one of my works inspired by the master: *THE ARROW*.

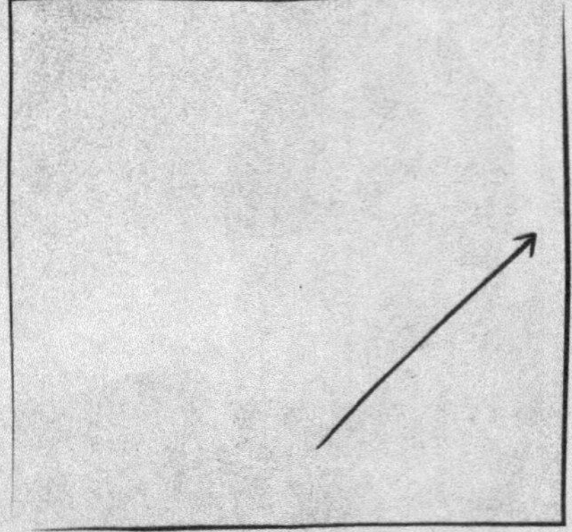

It's powerful art, I think you'll agree and my latest one was even better. I snuck it into the centenary edition of *Taskmaster*. These are my favourite episodes, *when I was a good boy*.

In my youth I travelled to New York to see Mondrian's work close up. I found my bearings in a damp hotel where West 43rd meets 9th. It would have been on the top floor, on the left. And from there I visited no fewer than four sites to find my answer: First, *One Times Square* because it sounded like one of his pictures; nothing. Next, *The Empire State Building* because back then it was still the world's second tallest building (as always, they're the ones I notice); again, nothing. Onto *The Morgan Library and Museum* because it was nearby and sounded official; nothing. And then finally, my one remaining hope, *The Honduran Consulate*; again, bizarrely, nothing.

I went home disappointed. But then I remembered the Museum of Modern Art so I went to New York a second time exactly a year later and had my fill. I always recommend going back and trying again. There it was; his masterpiece; the beautifully titled *Composition with Red, Yellow and Blue, 1942*. I stopped and stared for hours, the *yellow block* particularly inspiring me.

After being thrown out of the gallery for lingering, I stood up straighter, wiser, and brushed the dirt off my shoulders. I learnt that day that I can make it. It may be expensive and painful but if I keep trying I can rise to the top, just like Mondrian.

Unfortunately for me, the path to the crown has been made clear to me and it turns out the title does not go from Taskmaster to Taskmaster's Assistant. It was ordained many years ago, at a drinks party after series one in fact, that the next in line to the slightly larger throne is actually The Task… Consultant.

So first I must either replace or dispose of That Man. This is not an easy task. But I will persist and keep trying. In the end, that's the most important thing to do.

The Taskmaster Assistant's Wisdom:

'Habitually observe accomplices'

Tasks
for larger
parties

TASK #41

Draw, from memory, the following things.

Best representation of each thing wins.

You will have one minute per thing.

Your time starts when your Taskmaster says each thing.

Your Taskmaster will only say the list once so you must remember the things then remember the things:

1. The British Rail symbol

2. Noel Edmonds

3. The T-junction sign

4. The cover of Pink Floyd's *Dark Side Of The Moon*

5. All the vital organs

6. The computer keyboard

7. Scandinavia

8. A maple leaf

9. The Citroen emblem

10. Sunday roast chicken

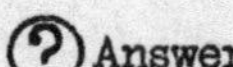

Clue #41

Red.
Blue.
Yellow.
Green

Answer ....

TASK #42

Draw the same picture as your Taskmaster.

You may not look at your Taskmaster's picture and you must all draw at the same time.

Your Taskmaster will draw something that consists of:

The head of their favourite animal.

The top half of their favourite building.

The underwear they are currently wearing.

The bottom half of either a bird, a fish or an insect.

And this creature is sitting on something that your Taskmaster finds very funny.

Closest to your Taskmaster's picture wins.

Clue #42

I played Lennie, one of Dan and Edna's granddaughters.

Answer ....

TASK #43

Everyone must get a mug 3/4 full of water then your Taskmaster can read the following task:

Hide your mug of water on your person.

You may not swallow any of the water or pour out any of the water apart from onto yourself.

Your Taskmaster will lock themselves in the toilet for five minutes.

On their return they will try to locate ANY water on each of you from a distance of two metres.

Most wrong guesses wins.

Clue #43

♩ = 118

3

Answer ....

TASK #44

PART ONE

Hold something yellow above your head. Fastest wins.

PART TWO

Balance your yellow thing on your head. Fastest wins.

PART THREE

Break your yellow thing into three equal pieces. Fastest wins.

PART FOUR

Phone someone not in this room and tell them what your yellow thing was. Fastest wins.

PART FIVE

Draw a recognisable picture of your yellow thing on your foot[1]. Fastest wins.

[1] Note

PART SIX

Hold an exact copy of your original yellow thing, but in blue, above your head. Fastest wins.

PART SEVEN

Repeat the steps (moving on to red, green, black, white and brown), until you find your winner.

Clue #44

B, D, D, G, H, S, ? (in full)

Answer ....

TASK #45

One by one, go outside and take a photo of a single thing.

You have one minute each.

Anyone who takes the same picture as someone else wins a point.

If there's any hint of communication the communicators lose all their points in this task.

Do this five times.

Most points wins.

Clue #45

This is an acknowledgement that in 2007 we found Hassan between 20th and 30th, but where was Hassan from?

Answer ....

TASK #46

The person wearing the brightest item must pass an item of clothing to the person on their right.

That person must pass an item of their clothing to their right, but they may not pass something that has been passed to them.

If you refuse you are out.

Last person to refuse, or run out of clothes, loses.

Your time starts now.

Clue #46

Break the seal at puzzlepost.com. I'D use Taskmaster.

Answer ....

TASK #47

PART ONE

Go and get a book.

You have two minutes.

Your time starts now.

PART TWO

Select a page in your book.

You have thirty seconds.

Your time starts now.

PART THREE

Do the following things (right).

The best at each one gets one point.

You have one minute for each one unless otherwise stated.

Find the longest word beginning with T.

Find the rudest sentence.

Find the silliest name.

Find the most 'x's.

Find the most confusing sentence.

Find a word that your Taskmaster doesn't understand.

Find a palindrome. Fastest wins.

Sing a sentence and make it sound like a line from a song. Highest page number wins.

Find two words with five or more letters that rhyme. Fastest wins.

Tell a story among your group, picking a word at a time from your book. You are disqualified if you hesitate too long or don't make sense.

Clue #47

Uh oh, it's a hospital heist in a book! And there are fifty three of these things lined up in a big sleepy burglary, just like parliament. If you need help, ask the Radio 1 Breakfast host. He wrote it.

Answer ....

TASK #48

PART ONE

Find the oldest photo on your phone and show it to your Taskmaster.

You have four minutes.

Your time starts now.

PART TWO

Recreate the old photo you found.

Best recreation wins.

You have four minutes.

Your time starts now.

Clue #48

I am six times longer than the Amazon, a fifth of me is dry and the rest is wet.

Answer ....

TASK #49

Your Taskmaster must get a cookery book and open it randomly on a recipe. They will read out the recipe but miss out ten crucial words or numbers.

Guess the missing words from the recipe.

Most correct answers wins.

You have three minutes.

Your time starts now.

This task can be repeated with DIY manuals, nature books, sports books, joke books and children's stories.

Clue #49

Salt, vegetable juice concentrate, vitamins, natural flavouring and what? Your pa won't get this but...

Answer ....

TASK #50

Take it in turn to pretend to do the following things.

Most realistic attempts, in your Taskmaster's opinion, wins:

1. **Laugh**
2. **Sneeze**
3. **Yawn**
4. **Angry Outburst**
5. **Quack**
6. **Faint**
7. **Witness a robbery**
8. **Go to sleep**
9. **Win the lottery**
10. **Put something in an envelope, seal the envelope, write the address, buy some stamps, post the letter**

Clue #50

I get on the London Underground in zone 9 and travel east for 12 stops. I change lines and travel south until the third stop after I've gone under the river, then change lines. I go south for five stops then change lines. North for three stops. West for four. It's 8 o clock. It's the 1st July 1973. I joined in with the encore because it's my favourite song. But what number did this song get to in the US charts?

Answer ....

TASK #51

PART ONE

Draw an animal with your wrong hand.

You have three minutes.

Your time starts now.

PART TWO

Disguise your animal using five straight lines (drawn with your correct hand).

Best disguised animal wins.

You have three minutes.

Taskmaster is a particularly subjective gameshow. There are often not clear winners. Instead it comes down to the judgment of a big man who can sometimes be short-tempered and wrong. Ideally, your Taskmaster will judge your disguised animals in exactly the same way.

Clue #51

The surname of the winner of the first season of the first top flight football team to play Taskmaster.

Answer ....

TASK #52

Each contestant should pick a number between 1 and 10 then the Taskmaster should read out the following:

Gather the most items.

Your items must all fill into the category that you have just chosen.

You have three minutes.

Your time starts when your Taskmaster bellows "go go gathering!"

1. Lids (separated from containers)

2. Unusual hats

3. Teeth related items

4. Different purple things

5. Types of cream

6. Pictures of chickens

7. Brushes

8. Hexagons

9. Sort of roundish wooden things

10. Battery operated items

Clue #52

Nathan was first to complete all the tasks in the first *Taskmaster* book. What word did he make up in the process?

Answer ....

TASK #53

Your Taskmaster should hand out peas and potatoes, or the closest to these things that are available:

Make the best pea shooter or spud gun.

You must demonstrate your pea shooter or spud gun in eight minutes from now.

Clue #53

Th frst wrd lk ths n ths pltfrm.

Answer ....

TASK #54

Gather the most fluff and dust.

You may not go within two metres of a tumble dryer or vacuum cleaner.

You have five minutes.

Your time starts now.

Clue #54

What was I doing in the eighth wordgame of *Countdown* two weeks and one day before my 30th birthday?

Answer ....

TASK #55

Everyone must each go to a different room in the house and fully close the door. You may not be in the same room as someone else. If there are not enough rooms you may use the front, back and sides of the house.

Your Taskmaster will then text everyone the following five tasks:

Make a portrait of your Taskmaster out of things in your room.

Best portrait wins.

You have three minutes to text your Taskmaster your portrait.

Your time starts now.

Clue #55

The answer to my fiendish riddle just before Mike brought in a spoon.

Answer ....

TASK #56

Your Taskmaster will shout your name.

When you hear your name you must shout back.

The person whom your Taskmaster hears clearest wins.

Clue #56

Chevy plays this on my song.

Answer ....

TASK #57

Hide.

You must stay in your room.

Your Taskmaster will go into each of the rooms in turn and start the clock on entry.

The person who is found after the longest time wins.

Clue #57

This word sounds the same when you lop off the final four fifths.

Answer ....

TASK #58

Change your outfit.

Your new outfit must consist entirely of things found in your room.

You must be wearing your new outfit when your Taskmaster summons you back to their room.

You have five minutes.

Your time starts now.

Clue #58

Elsewhere you can see him exiting a pet shop, in a newspaper advert and carrying a double bass. But in which film would you find him wearing a cowboy hat as Marion passes by on her way in?

Answer ....

TASK #59

Return to your Taskmaster's room.

You must be carrying the most important item.

Most important item wins.

You must say "I'm back, baby" to your Taskmaster within two minutes from now.

Clue #59

This James never said hello to me.

Answer ....

TASK #60

Go and get ten things beginning with consecutive letters of the alphabet.

You have five minutes.

Your time starts now.

THEN DO THE FOLLOWING FOUR TASKS USING YOUR THINGS:

Make a tower using just your things.

Highest tower wins.

You have three minutes.

Your time starts now.

Clue #60

T 7th P F T S (cheeky)

Answer ....

TASK #61

Make a limerick mentioning at least half of your things.

Best limerick wins.

You have three minutes.

Your time starts now.

Clue #61

sVI elV: TITLE

Answer ....

TASK #62

Makes a disaster film on your phone using your things.

Best disaster film wins.

You have five minutes.

Your time starts now.

Clue #62

? _ _ _ _ _ _ tree
? _ _ _ _ _ coffee
to _ _ _ _ _ _ _ _ _ _ _ _ _ knees
come _ _ _ _ _ _ _ _ _ melody

Answer ....

TASK #63

Throw all your things into a welly that your Taskmaster will place in the middle of the room.

Each player must throw something in turn.

Most things in the welly at the end wins.

Clue #63

Double Double Toad and Puzzle: Can you escape? And if so, what is the prince called?

Answer ....

TASK #64

Go and get a cuddly toy that looks like you.

The cuddly toy that looks most like their finder wins.

You have three minutes.

Your time starts now.

Clue #64

The seventh champion had a chat with #59 and the ninth champion and she thinks apples would be better if they were the size of these things.

Answer ....

TASK #65

Make a parachute for your cuddly toy that looks like you.

You have ten minutes after which your Taskmaster will throw them all out of a window.

Best parachute wins.

Your time starts now.

Clue #65

Who recommended the neck of a goose?

Answer ....

TASK #66

PART ONE

Write down the titles of ten songs.

You have three minutes.

Your time starts now.

PART TWO

Take it in turns to describe your songs to your Taskmaster.

You may not use any of the words from the title of the song, you may not sing the tune and you may not name the band.

You have three minutes each.

Most songs guessed by your Taskmaster wins.

But also, if any of your songs are the same as anyone else's songs you all lose a point for those songs.

Clue #66

The shape of the island 1425 kilometres south-east from Big Ben.

Answer ....

TASK #67

PART ONE

Everyone must write down:

(a) A number between 1 and 100

(b) A number between 1 and 10

(c) A number between 1 and 20

(d) A number between 1 and 50

(e) A number between 1 and 5

PART TWO

Draw (a) monsters with (b) legs and (c) eyes then do (d) star jumps.

You have (e) minutes.

Your time starts now.

Clue #67

- Author
- Comedian
- Contestant
- First novel clue
- Surname?

Answer ....

TASK #68

Your Taskmaster should go and get a map or atlas. Your Taskmaster should pick a city, but not say it yet.

Guess your Taskmaster's city.

Closest city to your Taskmaster's city wins.

Your Taskmaster should then describe a journey from that first city to another city of their choice, using things like directions, distances, clues and whatever else they want to involve.

Guess where your Taskmaster has travelled to.

Closest to the correct destination wins.

Clue #68

What you get if you pour a blue slushy on a cuddly toy, innit.

Answer ....

TASK #69

Name a country beginning with the same letter as your name.

Your Taskmaster must also name a country beginning with the same letter as their name.

Now write down:

The capital of your country.

A neighbouring country to your country (or the closest one if yours is an island).

The distance between your country and the Taskmaster's country.

The flag of your country.

And finally:

Write a brand new national anthem for your country.

Most correct answers and best anthem wins.

Clue #69

Our newsreader's favourite word.

Answer ....

TASK #70

One by one, go into the bathroom and take a photo of a part of your body.

Your photo must be in focus.

When you have all returned you have to stand up and tell your Taskmaster what part of the body it is.

Your Taskmaster will say whether they think you are telling the truth.

If they get it right you must sit down.

Last person standing wins.

Clue #70

I am nearly 343mm tall and I weigh 3856g.

Answer ....

TASK #71

If you are over forty, dress up as someone forty years younger than you.

If you are under forty, dress up as someone forty years older than you.

Most convincing older or younger person wins.

You have ten minutes.

Your time starts now.

Clue #71

The tenth champion and I had a chat in Leicester Square and it turned out he paid £39 more than me for his one of these.

Answer ....

TASK #72

This one requires a bit of preparation. Your Taskmaster('s assistant, probably) will need to have made a lot of mince pies but filled them with things other than mince (like toothpaste, Chinese Five Spice, egg, extra strong mints, marmite, mustard, lettuce, crisps, a tomato, cheese, the other sort of mince).

Work out what is in the mince pies without looking inside the mince pies.

You have ten minutes.

Most correct guesses wins.

Clue #72

Tell me two of the 'B's in LBBB and we'll forget all about it.

Answer ....

TASK #73

Put the most good things in a sock.

Whoever puts the most good things in a sock wins.

You have eight minutes.

Your time starts now.

Clue #73

The poet wrote a poem about this naughty man wearing a kilt the day after *Star Wars* Day.

Answer ....

TASK #74

PART ONE

Find a picture that you don't mind destroying and rip it into tiny pieces.

You have three minutes.

Your time starts now.

PART TWO

Put together the jigsaw you have just created.

Fastest wins.

Your time starts now.

Clue #74

Officially, 2019 looked like this: Olivia and Oliver, Amelia and George, Isla and Noah, Ava and Arthur, Mia and Harry, Isabella and Leo, Sophia and Muhammad, Grace and Jack, Lily and who?

Answer ....

Answer ....

TASK #75

Everyone must balance a coin on their head then one by one do the following:

Catch your coin in a mug below your waist.

You have ten attempts each.

Most catches wins.

Clue #75

Lion, boy, boys, boy, orange, ?, stick, dog, cockerel.

Answer ....

TASK #76

Write down the most words with four or more letters.

All your words must start and end with a vowel.

Also, you must all hum throughout.

Most correct words wins.

You have three minutes.

Your time starts now.

Clue #76

$\text{Blue}_{\text{Yellow}}{}^{(\,)}{}_{\text{Green}}{}^{\text{Red}}$, Sp Su Au ( ), Ti ( ) Re

Buscemi, Daltrey, Moore

Gos, Black, Fish

Toschi (07), The Narrator (99), Chopper (00)

Pig, Flat, Grid

Kavanagh, Regan, Morse

Answer ....

TASK #77

You must all leave the room for three minutes then, one by one, pass the most sinister thing under the door to the Taskmaster.

Most sinister thing passed under the door wins.

You must leave the room now.

Clue #77

Stand up and look in the mirror. Stretch your arms out to the side. Spread your legs apart, put your elbows on your knees and shake hands with yourself. Do a star jump. Cross your legs and put your hands in your pockets.

Answer ....

TASK #78

PART ONE

(Do not read part two until part one is complete).

Everyone must secretly write down the name of another player.

You have thirty seconds.

Your time starts now.

PART TWO

Without anyone seeing the name you wrote, draw a portrait of your person on another piece of paper.

You must hold your pen in your mouth throughout.

You have three minutes.

Any face recognised by the Taskmaster wins five points.

Your time starts now.

Clue #78

There's a big one @NZ2774.

Answer ....

TASK #79

Draw a picture on a piece of paper then rip out holes and put parts of your body through the holes.

Most entertaining final picture wins.

You have three minutes.

Your time starts now.

Clue #79

Penelope Pitstop wears these on her hands according to one of the jockeys.

TASK #80

When your Taskmaster says so, everyone must leave the room.

When your Taskmaster calls you back in, your Taskmaster will have put some things from the room in a bag.

Without touching or inspecting the bag, guess how many things your Taskmaster has put in the bag, and what the things are.

You will have two minutes to work out what, from the room, is in the bag.

Closest answers wins.

Clue #80

Tony

Dion

Tyrone

Tom

?

John

Paul

Albert

Answer ....

THE STARTER

We were all babies and one day, we were all born. It happened to you, it happened to me. It happened to every single person you've ever seen. We were all once tiny naked crying people.

Some of these people were born to lead, others to run and about a dozen to be truly wild. Maybe you were born to dance. More likely you were born to sometimes jog quite slowly, often walk about a bit and mostly sit down a lot. Back in 1978, I was not born to do any of those things. I was born to assist.

The middle of three boys, I grew up in a world where I sat happily in second place. I was happy not to have to try things first, or indeed last. I was comfortable following.

My childhood consisted of setting up games, as my adulthood would too. I was the one who set up the *Monopoly* board, dished out the money and organised the cards. I'd even move the counters for everyone, with GO always at my bottom left; "*a five from Whitechapel, up to Chance*; You have won a crossword competition – collect £100! There's your money…".

For me, the best games have clear rules with idiosyncratic sub-laws. I've always loved the intricacies of cricket, for instance, even though I was never that good at the actual sport, averaging just 25.30 runs like one of my heroes. But I've been known to be diverted by any competitive pastime, no matter how minor.

With *Battleships* I played the role of a nautical referee, checking coordinates, notifying players if their boats were hit with sound effects and actions. I was a stickler for the rules and terms: the Destroyer occupied two spaces, a Cruiser five. "Three strikes! Submarine down!" My favourite, the actual *Battleship* took up four. Years later I recorded a music video featuring that particular vessel and can still remember *exactly where I placed it* to defeat my 10 year old foe.

It's perhaps no surprise I now make up games of my own (for Him, of course). I was and always have been obsessed. I'd play *Tetris* for hours, working out mathematical strategies to ensure my *T Tetronimo never landed point first on the left hand side*. Simple riddles hooked me too. I loved my old *Gardener's Word Search Puzzle book* (and the new version by the Master Puzzlers is definitely worth a look, although you do need to consult *VAR* nowadays).

Those innocent grids always lured me in, with the best ones containing every letter of the alphabet at least once. *Some even sheltered words that weren't in a straight line!* You had to do your homework to find the answers, but when you did, boy was it worth it.

So, forty-three years after my arrival, I made you this, the second *Taskmaster* book, another chance for you to take part in tasks for Him, to test yourselves and others and to discover what you were born to do.

As well as the one hundred and one tasks, there is also this second, larger task in the form of a pesky puzzle to solve. Some of you will be spending hours, days, weeks and months racking your brains, trying to figure out the answers. Others won't bother. The wild ones will either burn or eat their books. But my advice to those of you who are still trying to complete the ultimate task is simply this: take your time. There's no rush. It's ok to have a second look and to follow others.

And I shall assist you. I shall be your second in command.

There is a page on the taskmaster.tv website where you can enter your responses to check if they're right. I'm not a monster. I'm an assistant. So, keep going. You can get 100% on this test. Every answer is a single word. Well, nearly every answer. Two are two words and one is two letters, because as the second son I know how important the number two is.[2]

But yes, you're mainly looking for simple one word answers.

And then there's the grid after Task #101. That's yours to fill in as you see fit. If I were you I'd use a pencil, but that's an enormous if. I'm just saying that you may well not get it right on your first go. But you will know you've got it when you look at numbers 26 to 30.

Having filled it in correctly, you'll need to work out what to do next. It won't be easy. You will almost certainly need a second look at this **Starter** as well as taking a few more bites of the **Apple**. Even when you've found what you're looking for, you'll still have one more clue to solve. That's the end of the **Endgame**. I mentioned cricket earlier; at the end of the day there are thirteen crucial characters on the pitch and your job is to watch them until they're finished, even the old Lancashire stalwart at backward point.

I know this is fiddly stuff. But, in celebration of their glory, every time Chesham United win a league game by two goals or more following this book's publication, I'll reveal one more hint on Twitter. So follow me as I follow Him and the Generals. We'll get there. In the words of the great *(ten letter) Lan O'Gaid*:

"Primo pessimus. Secundum optimum. Tertio unum vertices capilli perambulantium in pectore."

Have fun. Be kind. Make good choices.

---

[2] By the way, it's worth you knowing how important the number 2 is too. You should by now know the last two numbers between one and a hundred, alphabetically, for instance. I've told you that twice.

Die Weisheit des Taskmaster-Assistenten:

'Nacktschnecke! Absacker! Schweinehund!'

Zoom Tasks

SOME ZOOM TASK EXPLANATION

Here are some tasks to keep you going if you want to host a *Taskmaster* evening over Zoom or Teams but probably Zoom. Despite it being forced upon us for so long, I do like Zoom. I was tempted to post an open Zoom invite here – Meeting: ID 827 5627 837 Passcode: 442130, for instance. But that seems like too much of an open goal.

Zoom works weirdly well for *Taskmaster* events, I suppose because the challenges in the show have also been done by the contestants in isolation. With Zoom, families or individuals also have to tackle the tasks by themselves, letting themselves down and embarrassing themselves as much as they want, without seeing how the others are getting on, while your Taskmaster can do all the judging without leaving their comfortable chair.

All you have to do is appoint your Taskmaster who will hand out points throughout the event, then send round Zoom invites and a couple of preparatory instructions. For example, your Taskmaster might ask their contestants to arrive on the Zoom in one of the following ways:

1. Wearing the most sophisticated outfits
2. Wearing the most surprising outfits
3. Dressed as a famous person; best outfit wins
4. Dressed as a character from a film; best outfit wins
5. Dressed as a historical figure: best outfit wins
6. Wearing the spookiest clothes
7. Dressed how you would dress 30/20/10 years ago
8. Dressed as something beginning with the letter T (or any letter of your choice!): best outfit wins

9. Wearing action clothes. Best action clothes wins
10. Wearing the most inappropriate clothing. Most inappropriate clothing wins

Your Taskmaster might also tell people that they must provide an item for the prize pot. Whoever emerges victorious will be the proud owners of all these items. The prize category could be one of the following:

1. Best drinking vessel
2. Best framed picture
3. Best coat
4. Most pointless thing that looks nice
5. Most beautiful cheap thing
6. Best homemade item
7. The oldest thing that is also very useful
8. Nicest smelling thing that is bigger than a rabbit
9. The best outdoor thing
10. The best bathroom accessory

Of course, the players must not talk to each other about these items and should arrive on the Zoom call promptly and ceremoniously. Your Taskmaster will judge their outfits and prize items then crack on with whichever of the following tasks they fancy.

There are ten tasks you can then carry out here. If you'd like more, please head to the taskmaster.tv website where there's a video you can buy and for which all funds go to the Homeless Link charity. Finally, almost all of the tasks in this book can be adapted for Zoom *Taskmaster* sessions, so please have a play.

TASK #81

Show me a completely peeled piece of fruit that isn't a banana.

Fastest wins.

Your time starts now.

Clue #81

Yes, I'm on the table and I'm 39.

Answer ....

TASK #82

Make it look like you are underwater.

Most realistic underwater scene wins.

You may not change your Zoom background.

You have four minutes.

Your time starts now.

Clue #82

This festival is a narrow strip of land that follows a condensed Costa Rica.

Answer ....

TASK #83

Put on a hat, sunglasses, a scarf, gloves and a stripy top then hold up a picture of an elephant that you haven't drawn and that isn't digital.

Fastest wins.

Clue #83

Which year connects us? Maria Callas, Julie Andrews, Kiki Dee, Kirsty MacColl, Missy Elliott, Amy Winehouse.

Answer ....

TASK #84

Draw an alien.

The monster with the *third* most eyes wins.

There is a bonus point for the best alien.

You have three minutes.

Your time starts now.

Clue #84

H, S, K A T, K A T.
H, S, K A T, K A T
A E A E A M A N.
H, S, K A T, ? A T. (in full)

Answer ....

TASK #85

Put the most shoes in saucepans.

Most shoes in saucepans wins.

You have two minutes.

Your time starts now.

Clue #85

-.-..-.-..--..-.-.-.- (cvccvcc – sorry there are no spaces)

Answer ....

TASK #86

Make a picture of a famous naughty person out of things from your kitchen.

Best picture of a famous naughty person wins.

You have three minutes.

Your time starts now.

Clue #86

It's a huge plus that this is the only toxic Joe Blake in Britain.

Answer ....

TASK #87

Bring back a book with a picture of a rainbow in.

Fastest wins.

Your time starts now.

Clue #87

Face south. Spin 180 degrees clockwise, then 270 degrees to your left. Now spin 180 degrees anti-clockwise and 270 degree to your right. Turn your head 45 degrees to the right. Aim your eyes another 30 degrees to the right. Do a 630 degree spin to the left. Shut your eyes. Spin 45 degrees clockwise. Open your eyes. You are now looking directly south. Where are you?

Answer ....

TASK #88

Dress up as either the Loch Ness Monster or a cheerleader.

Best Loch Ness Monster or cheerleader wins.

You have five minutes.

Your time starts now.

Feel free to add your own dressing up options.

Clue #88

tail (cat)
eye eye eye eye
neck neck neck neck neck neck neck
head head head head head head
tentacle tentacle tentacle tentacle tentacle tentacle tentacle tentacle tentacle tentacle tentacle tentacle
tooth (shark)

Answer ....

TASK #89

Line up ten objects.

The objects must each begin with different letters and those letters must spell out the words "I AM AMAZING".

Fastest wins.

Your time starts now.

Clue #89

A horse controls the ball in front of a gate by the sea.

Answer ....

TASK #90

Say your name the slowest.

Everyone should do this at the same time.

You must not take a breath.

You must be honest.

Last person still saying their name wins.

You must all start saying your name when your Taskmaster says their name.

Clue #90

9pm open brackets X multiplied by vermilion close brackets equals happy Ben.

Answer ....

The Taskmaster Assistant's Wisdom:

'Talk About Accessories'

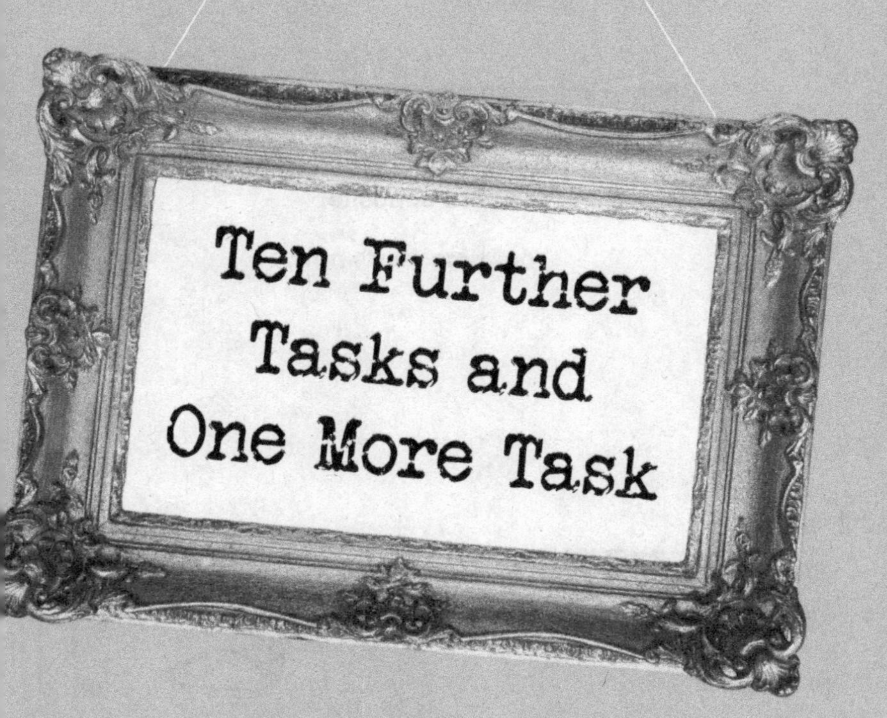
Ten Further
Tasks and
One More Task

TASK #91

Choose your own pieces and prescribe them your own special powers, then play your own version of chess with someone else on the board opposite.

Your time starts now.

Clue #91

We've all got one of these, but what is it?

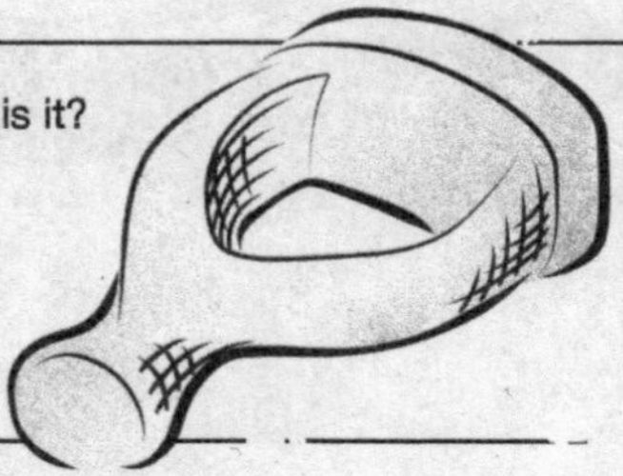

Answer ....

	A	B	C	D	E	F	G	H
1								
2								
3								
4								
5								
6								
7								
8								

TASK #92

Hide this page within a mile of your house then write a treasure map detailing exactly where it is.

Give this treasure map to someone you love.

Your time starts now.

Clue #92

One fine day to Chesham fair, he ventured forth to meet the mayor. But what did that mayor think his surname was?

Answer ....

TASK #93

Completely change the view from one of your windows.

Most spectacular change from before to after wins.

Your time starts now.

Clue #93

The organ hiding in King James' Exodus 30:25.

Answer ....

TASK #94

Make the best butterfly face version of your own face on the pages after this one.

You must pour paint or ink onto one page then close the book to make your face.

Your time starts now.

Clue #94

Johnny, Ronnie, John, Ron, Ronnie, Ron, Johnny, Nobby, Ron, Ron, ?

Answer ....

TASK #95

Make an enormous pair of legs and demonstrate them in action.

Most enormous working legs win.

Your time starts now.

Clue #95

Apple, pears, plums, ?, oranges, chocolate cake etc.

Answer ....

TASK #96

Turn a bath into something far more exciting than a bath.

Most exciting non-bath bath wins.

Your time starts now.

Clue #96

My little trumpeter plays in this band while the fifth champion listens on his island.

Answer ....

TASK #97

Fly.

You may not do anything dangerous.

Best flight wins.

Your time starts now.